Tools

Search

Notes

Discuss

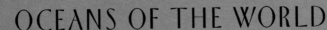
MyReportLinks.com Books

Go!

OCEANS OF THE WORLD

THE PACIFIC OCEAN

A MyReportLinks.com Book

DOREEN GONZALES

MyReportLinks.com Books

an imprint of
Enslow Publishers, Inc.
Box 398, 40 Industrial Road
Berkeley Heights, NJ 07922
USA

MyReportLinks.com Books, an imprint of Enslow Publishers, Inc. MyReportLinks®
is a registered trademark of Enslow Publishers, Inc.

Library of Congress Cataloging-in-Publication Data

Gonzales, Doreen.
  The Pacific Ocean / Doreen Gonzales.
     p. cm. — (Oceans of the world)
Summary: Describes the physical characteristics, plant and animal life,
explorers, and environmental problems of the world's largest ocean, the
Pacific. Includes Internet links to web sites related to oceans.
Includes bibliographical references and index.
  ISBN 0-7660-5192-7
  1. Oceanography—Pacific Ocean—Juvenile literature. 2. Pacific
Ocean—Juvenile literature. [1. Pacific Ocean. 2. Oceanography.] I.
Title.
  GC771.G66 2004
  551.46'14—dc22
                                        2003014397

Printed in the United States of America

10 9 8 7 6 5 4 3 2 1

To Our Readers:
Through the purchase of this book, you and your library gain access to the Report Links that specifically back
up this book.
The Publisher will provide access to the Report Links that back up this book and will keep these Report Links
up to date on **www.myreportlinks.com** for three years from the book's first publication date.
We have done our best to make sure all Internet addresses in this book were active and appropriate when we
went to press. However, the author and the Publisher have no control over, and assume no liability for, the
material available on those Internet sites or on other Web sites they may link to.
The usage of the MyReportLinks.com Books Web site is subject to the terms and conditions stated on the
Usage Policy Statement on **www.myreportlinks.com**.
A password may be required to access the Report Links that back up this book. The password is found on the
bottom of page 4 of this book.
Any comments or suggestions can be sent by e-mail to comments@myreportlinks.com or to the address on
the back cover.

Photo Credits: Central Array of Relayed Transaction for the Advance of General Education, p. 36;
© Corel Corporation, pp. 16, 25, 30, 31, 38, 42; Copyright ©1996, 1997, 1998 by The Mariners'
Museum, p. 34; © 1996–2003 National Wildlife Federation, p. 21; © 2003 Extreme Science, p. 19;
Dr. James P. McVey, National Oceanic and Atmospheric Administration, p. 18; *Exxon Valdez* Oil Spill
Trustee Council, p. 40; Jamie Hall, National Oceanic and Atmospheric Administration, p. 32; Kip
Evans, National Oceanic and Atmospheric Administration, pp. 24, 27; MyReportLinks.com Books,
p. 4; National Oceanic and Atmospheric Administration, pp. 12, 22; Photos.com, pp. 1, 3, 9, 28; Scot
Anderson, National Oceanic and Atmospheric Administration, p. 26; Stan Butler, National Oceanic
and Atmospheric Administration, p. 17; U.S. Army Service Forces, Army Specialized Training
Division, p. 14.

Cover Photo: © Corel Corporation

Cover Description: California surfer

Contents

MyReportLinks.com Books
Great Books, Great Links, Great for Research!

The Report Links listed on the following four pages can save you hours of research time by **instantly** bringing you to the best Web sites relating to your report topic.

How to Use MyReportLinks.com

1 Got a Report to do?

2 Check out a MyReportLinks.com Book at the Library.

3 Read the Book.

4 Go to www.myreportlinks.com for Quick, Safe, and Up-to-Date Links!

5 Internet Report Links = Great Information.

6 Write Your Report. Impress Your Teacher.

MAX LYNX

The pre-evaluated Web sites are your links to source documents, photographs, illustrations, and maps. They also provide links to dozens—even hundreds—of Web sites about your report subject.

MyReportLinks.com Books and the MyReportLinks.com Web site save you time and make report writing easier than ever!

Please see "To Our Readers" on the copyright page for important information about this book, the MyReportLinks.com Web site, and the Report Links that back up this book. Please enter **OPA2801** if asked for a password.

Report Links

➤ The Internet sites described below can be accessed at
http://www.myreportlinks.com

*EDITOR'S CHOICE

▶ **The *World Factbook 2002*: Pacific Ocean**
This page from the Central Intelligence Agency's *World Factbook*
contains a brief overview of the Pacific Ocean. Pacific geography,
economy, transportation, and transnational issues are covered here.

*EDITOR'S CHOICE

▶ **Deepest Place in the Ocean: Challenger Deep**
The Mariana Trench is the deepest trench in the world. The bottom of
the trench, named Challenger Deep, is 38,635 feet below sea level, the
lowest point on Earth. Here you will find information about the trench,
how it was formed, and its exploration.

*EDITOR'S CHOICE

▶ ***Savage Earth*: The Ring of Fire**
Over three fourths of the earth's volcanic activity occurs in a zone
around the Pacific Ocean known as the Ring of Fire. This page from
PBS's *Savage Earth* has information about this infamous volcanic zone.

*EDITOR'S CHOICE

▶ **Ocean World**
This site from Texas A&M University's College of Geosciences
contains a wealth of information about the study of the world beneath
the waves. Here you can learn about currents, waves, El Niño,
fisheries, coral reefs, and much more.

*EDITOR'S CHOICE

▶ **Pacific Ocean**
The ocean bottom, water characteristics, climate, geology, landmasses,
history, and the economy of the Pacific Ocean are covered. Links
within the text take you to other pages about such topics as the
Marianas Trench, seamounts, and James Cook.

*EDITOR'S CHOICE

▶ **Ocean Explorer**
The Ocean Explorer Web site contains information on the National
Oceanic and Atmospheric Administration's exploration activities.
Here you can also learn a great deal about oceanography, scientific
technology, the history of exploration, and much more.

Report Links

The Internet sites described below can be accessed at http://www.myreportlinks.com

▶ **All About Hawaii**

Located in the Pacific Ocean, Hawaii became the fiftieth state of the United States on August 21, 1959. On the official Hawaii Web site, you can learn about this island paradise.

▶ **American Museum of Natural History Expeditions: Black Smokers**

At this site from the American Museum of Natural History you can read about a mission to the bottom of the Pacific Ocean to learn about black smokers. These are spots in the ocean floor containing very hot water full of minerals.

▶ **Ancient Seafarers**

Recent archeological studies offer evidence of ancient sea crossings in the Pacific. In this article from *Archaeology* magazine, you can read about these new findings.

▶ **Dive and Discover**

The Woods Hole Oceanographic Institution operates a group of vehicles designed for deep-sea exploration. Their interactive Dive and Discover site allows you to accompany scientists in their exploration of the seafloor.

▶ **El Niño Theme Page**

El Niño and La Niña are disruptions of the ocean-atmosphere system. Here you will find El Niño and La Niña facts, forecasts, and more. The site is illustrated with animations and graphics.

▶ ***Exxon Valdez* Oil Spill Trustee Council**

The *Exxon Valdez* is an oil ship that, on March 23, 1989, spilled over 10 million gallons of crude oil into Prince William Sound. Learn about the accident and what has been done to clean it up.

▶ **Ferdinand Magellan**

Ferdinand Magellan was the first European explorer to sail across the Pacific, and his expedition was the first to circle the globe. Learn about Magellan and his pioneering voyage.

▶ **James Cook**

James Cook made three voyages on the Pacific Ocean in search of an unknown southern continent. Biographical information on this legendary navigator is included.

Any comments? Contact us: **comments@myreportlinks.com**

Report Links

The Internet sites described below can be accessed at http://www.myreportlinks.com

▶**Mountains Under the Sea**
At the National Wildlife Federation Web site you can read an article about seamounts located in the Pacific Ocean.

▶**NASA Visible Earth: Pacific Ocean**
View dozens of satellite images of the Pacific Ocean on NASA's Visible Earth Web site. Typhoons, hurricanes, cyclones, El Niño, and La Niña are among the events photographed from space.

▶**NOAA: Pacific Marine Environmental Laboratory**
The NOAA's Pacific Marine Environmental Laboratory carries out oceanography and atmospheric science investigations in the Pacific. Here you will find information about El Niño, La Niña, underwater volcanoes, tsunamis, and more.

▶**North Pacific Ocean Theme Page**
The Pacific Marine Environmental Laboratory Web site provides information on the northern region of the Pacific Ocean.

▶**Northwestern Hawaiian Islands Coral Reef Ecosystem Reserve**
The Northwestern Hawaiian Islands Coral Reef Ecosystem Reserve is the United States' largest marine-protected area. Here you will learn about the complex ecosystem in the reef and what is being done to preserve it.

▶**Odyssey Expeditions Tropical Marine Biology Voyages**
This site contains general marine science educational resources from the Marine Biology Learning Center. The topics covered include coral reefs, marine ecology, oceanography, and mangroves.

▶**Pacific Seabird Group: PSG Gallery**
The Pacific Seabird Group is dedicated to the study and conservation of seabirds. The Seabird Gallery contains photographs of the Pacific birds.

▶**The Restless Sea**
You will find information about currents, tides, tidal currents, waves, swells, breakers, and tsunamis at this site from the United States Naval Meteorology and Oceanography Command.

Report Links

**The Internet sites described below can be accessed at
http://www.myreportlinks.com**

▶*Savage Seas*

The Web site for PBS's *Savage Seas* provides insight into the inner workings of oceans. The four sections cover such topics as waves, exploration of the deep, disasters at sea, and weather.

▶**Scripps Institution of Oceanography**

The Scripps Institution of Oceanography in San Diego has been performing marine science research for a century. Their site provides news and information about the institution and its research.

▶**Sea World: Corals and Coral Reefs**

This Sea World site contains a variety of information about many aspects of coral. You can even learn how to grow your own coral.

▶**Sierra Club: Population and Overfishing Factsheet**

Overfishing occurs when fish do not reproduce as fast as they are caught. This Sierra Club fact sheet provides an overview of the problem, its causes, and what is being done to solve it.

▶**Sustainable Seas Expeditions: Monterey Bay**

Monterey Bay National Marine Sanctuary is the second largest sanctuary in the world. This interactive *National Geographic* site contains information about the sanctuary and its plant and animal life.

▶*Trieste*

In 1960, Don Walsh and Jacques Piccard journeyed to the lowest-known point in the ocean, Challenger Deep. Their vehicle was a bathyscaphe designed by Piccard called *Trieste*. Here you will learn about seven of *Trieste*'s voyages.

▶**Tsunami!**

This site from the Geophysics Department at the University of Washington contains news and information about tsunamis and the Tsunami Warning System.

▶**WhaleNet**

This site is dedicated to whales and other marine mammals. Facts, tracking information, expedition accounts, images, maps, movies, and other resources are included.

Pacific Ocean Facts

Area

About 70 million square miles

About 181 million square kilometers

Average Depth

About 12,900 feet

About 3,900 meters

Greatest Known Depth

36,198 feet

11,033 meters

Place of Greatest Known Depth

Challenger Deep in the Mariana Trench

Greatest Distance

North-South: about 9,600 miles (15,450 kilometers)

East-West: about 15,00 miles (24,000 kilometers)

Surface Temperature

Highest: 82°F (28°C) near the equator.

Lowest: 30°F (–1°C) in the polar region during the winter season.

All metric and Celsius measurements used in this text are approximate estimates.

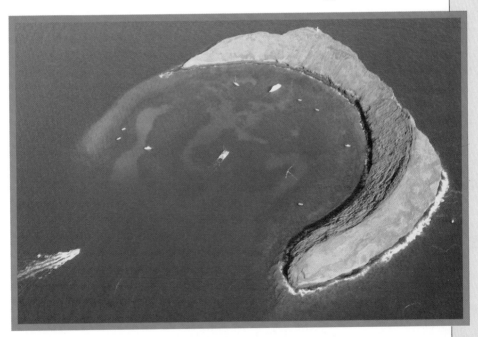

▲ The island of Molokini in Hawaii.

Chapter 1

THE EARTH'S LARGEST OCEAN

The Pacific Ocean is the largest ocean on Earth. It covers over 64 million square miles (166 million square kilometers). This is one third of the earth's surface.[1] The Pacific Ocean is so big that all of the world's land could float on top of it with room to spare.[2]

The Pacific Ocean stretches from the Arctic Circle in the north to the Southern Ocean in the south.[3] Asia and Australia form its western borders, and North and South America are its eastern boundaries. The Pacific is divided into two parts. The waters north of the equator are called

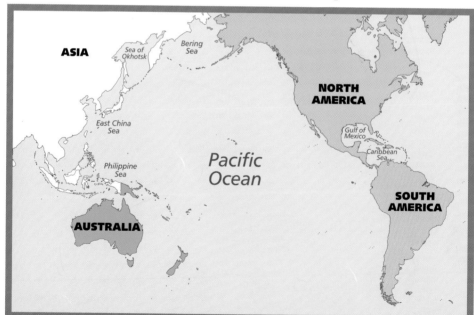

▲ A map of the Pacific Ocean.

the North Pacific. Those south of the equator are known as the South Pacific.

The Pacific holds several seas. Sea is another word for ocean. It can also mean a small part of an ocean. Pacific seas include the Bering Sea, Sea of Japan, South China Sea, and the Tasman Sea, among others.

More than twenty thousand islands dot the Pacific.[4] Almost all lie south of the equator.[5] Some are too small to live on, but the larger ones have been inhabited for centuries. Some, such as Japan and New Zealand, are independent countries. Others, like Hawaii and the Galapagos Islands, are part of a mainland country. The people who live on the Pacific Islands have many different cultures and languages.

Climate

The climate of the Pacific Ocean varies. The North Pacific has long, cold winters with short, cool summers. Along the equator, temperatures stay hot all year. This area is called the tropics. The South Pacific has cool winters and mild summers.

The water temperature in the Pacific Ocean also varies. Water near the equator is about 81°F (27°C).[6] In general, the farther the water is from the equator, the cooler its temperature. The temperature also drops as the water gets deeper. The water at the bottom of the ocean is just above freezing.[7]

The Pacific Ocean has two main currents. A current is like a river within the ocean. Currents are caused by wind and the earth's rotation. Pacific currents move in a circular pattern. One is in the North Pacific. It travels clockwise. The other main current is in the South Pacific. This one moves counterclockwise.

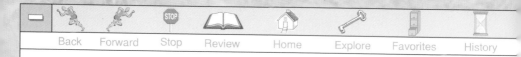

Currents act as giant heat regulators for the water and the land around the Pacific. As warm water from the equator circles the ocean, it releases its heat. This keeps temperatures in the far north and south from becoming extremely cold. Likewise, the cold water that flows to the equator from the north and south keep tropical temperatures from becoming too hot.

The air above the ocean is always moving, too. Ocean winds cause waves. The size of the waves depends on how hard and how long the wind blows. Some winds are predictable. Gentle winds called *trade winds* always blow

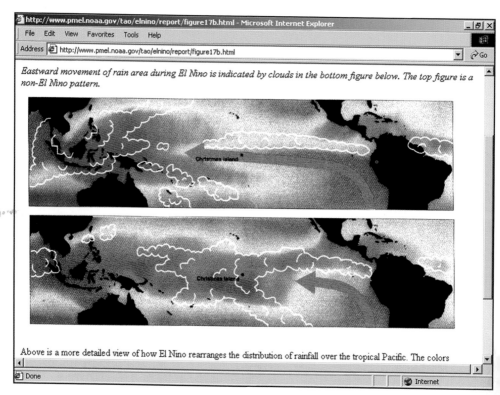

http://www.pmel.noaa.gov/tao/elnino/report/figure17b.html - Microsoft Internet Explorer

File   Edit   View   Favorites   Tools   Help

Address   http://www.pmel.noaa.gov/tao/elnino/report/figure17b.html   Go

Eastward movement of rain area during El Nino is indicated by clouds in the bottom figure below. The top figure is a non-El Nino pattern.

Above is a more detailed view of how El Nino rearranges the distribution of rainfall over the tropical Pacific. The colors

Done   Internet

▲ El Niño is the name of a major weather pattern that occurs in the Pacific Ocean. The top diagram indicates the normal distribution of rainfall in the Pacific, and the bottom diagram shows the amount of rainfall during El Niño.

Tools   Search   Notes   Discuss

toward the equator. Sailors once used them to travel across the Pacific. These winds can also be destructive. Typhoons and hurricanes begin in tropical waters. They have winds that whirl up to 150 miles (241 kilometers) per hour.

Many hurricanes stay over the ocean. They can capsize ships. Hurricanes that hit land can destroy homes and level large buildings. These storms are accompanied by heavy rains and high tides, which often cause floods.

Another Pacific weather system is called El Niño. El Niño happens when the water temperature in the South Pacific rises a few degrees. This minor change causes floods, storms, and droughts all around the world. El Niños happen every three to seven years. Each one lasts about a year.[8] Scientists do not know what causes El Niño. Therefore, they are not able to predict when one will occur.

El Niño is often followed by La Niña. During La Niña, the waters of the Pacific cool. Like El Niño, the temperature change of La Niña affects weather all over the planet.[9] It becomes abnormally warm or surprisingly cool in certain areas.

Tides

All Pacific waters have a tide. Tides are caused by the moon's gravity. It is always pulling water toward it. This causes each ocean wave that hits the shore to go a little farther onto land. When water has risen to its highest level, it is said to be at high tide. At this point, the earth and moon have changed position. The moon now pulls on different waters. Water that was rising begins receding. Water is at low tide when it has receded to its lowest point.

Wherever ocean meets land there are two high tides and two low tides each day. The islands in the middle of

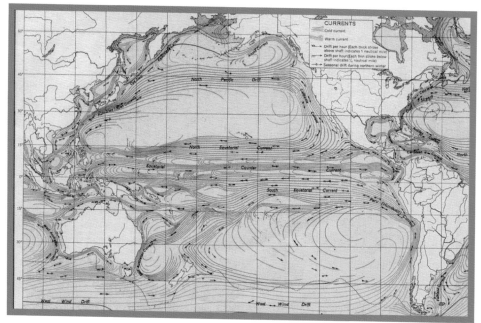

CURRENTS
Cold current
Warm current

△ This map shows the flow of the currents in the Pacific Ocean.

the Pacific have small tides. The difference between high and low tide there is less than a foot (thirty centimeters). Along the edges of the continents, though, the difference can be as much as thirty feet (nine meters).

▶ Water Cycle

The Pacific Ocean is vital to life on earth. Water from the ocean evaporates into the air. This vapor condenses, then falls to the ground as rain or snow. Much of the water is used by plants, animals, and people. The rest flows into rivers that run to the sea. Here the cycle begins again. Without the ocean's vast waters to keep this cycle going, we would have no water. Without water, life on earth could not survive.

OCEAN RESOURCES

The Pacific Ocean provides us with many resources. This includes food, substances such as oil and gas to produce energy, and metals and minerals. These valuable resources provide people with many products that aid their daily lives.

Food

Food is perhaps the most important of the Pacific Ocean's resources. Half of all the seafood eaten in the world comes from the Pacific.[1] For some people, seafood is just one of several foods they eat. For millions of others, though, seafood is the main source of protein in their diet. In addition, seaweed is an important food in certain countries. It is full of nutrients.

Energy

Oil and natural gas also come from the floor of the Pacific. These fuels power automobiles, airplanes, and machinery. They warm homes and schools.

Offshore wells must be built to obtain these fuels. An offshore well is a huge platform that stands on legs buried into the ocean floor. Pumps on top of the platform pull oil or gas from below the seafloor. Most Pacific offshore wells are near southeast Asia. There are also a few off the coast of California.

The Pacific may one day be used to create electric power. Power stations in other oceans use the rise and fall

▲ *When ocean water evaporates, it leaves behind salt granules. Salt can also be found deep below the seafloor. Sea salt is used for seasoning foods because it is full of natural flavor.*

of tides to turn generators and make electricity.[2] Certain experts believe there are places in the Pacific where tidal power plants could be built.[3]

▷ Minerals and Metals

Another resource that comes from the Pacific is salt. The waters of the Pacific Ocean are 2 to 3 percent salt. Salt is harvested by heating ocean water. When the water evaporates, salt is left behind.

The Pacific is also rich in manganese. This metal is used in making paints, batteries, and steel. Manganese lumps the size of potatoes cover miles of seafloor in some places.[4] Collecting these lumps, called nodules, is often expensive. Consequently, most of the ocean's manganese has not been mined.

Other Products

Several medicines come from marine life. Blood from the horseshoe crab, for example, is used to help doctors locate certain infections. They add the blood from the horseshoe crab to human blood, and the type of clotting it causes lets the doctor know an infection is present.

Algar and algin are substances found in seaweed. They are used to improve the texture of various foods and drugs. Sand and gravel taken from the seafloor are used to make concrete.

Services

The ocean is useful in other ways, too. Many people depend on it to earn a living. Some catch seafood to sell. Others work in a hotel, store, or restaurant that serves tourists visiting the Pacific.

Furthermore, the Pacific Ocean is the world's biggest highway. Cargo ships carry food, cars, and hundreds of

▲ Humpback whales can be found in every ocean, including the Pacific.

▲ The Hawaiian monk seal is one Pacific animal that has been the subject of scientific studies.

other products across the ocean. Tankers carry oil from one Pacific port to another. Military vessels travel the Pacific. So do people on vacation and business trips. Each year, millions of people flock to the Pacific's beaches. Some surf and fish for leisure. Others simply swim or tan themselves on the beach.

Research Laboratory

Oceanographers are scientists who study the ocean. They view the Pacific as the world's largest laboratory. Some research how the ocean affects the world's climate. Others try to learn how man's use of the ocean impacts the earth. Marine biologists study the plants and animals of the sea.

Scientists believe there are ocean resources they have yet to discover. Perhaps there is a sea organism that can cure cancer or AIDS.[5] Or maybe an ocean discovery will help us understand more about the earth's history. Indeed, the ocean's unknown resources may be just as valuable as the resources we take from it now.

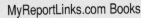
THE OCEAN FLOOR

The bottom of the Pacific Ocean slopes gently as it moves from the land toward the deep sea. This gradual incline is called a continental shelf. All of the earth's oceans have a continental shelf. The Pacific's shelf is narrow compared to the shelves in other oceans. It is only about one mile (one and one-half kilometers) long. At this point, the

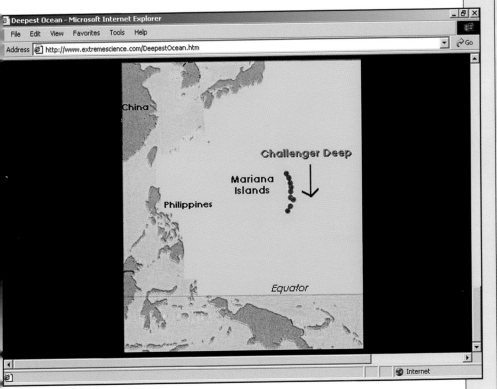

▲ The Mariana Trench, located in what is called Challenger Deep, is the deepest place in the Pacific. The tip of Mount Everest would not even surface the water if it were located within the trench.

seafloor drops sharply. The Pacific is the deepest ocean on Earth. Its average depth is 12,900 feet (3,932 meters).[1] Yet the bottom is not flat.

Trenches

Eighteen long, deep trenches gouge the bottom of the Pacific Ocean. The deepest is the Mariana Trench. Its lowest point lies 38,635 feet (11,776 meters) under the sea.[2] This is the deepest point on Earth. It is called Challenger Deep. The water pressure in Challenger Deep is immense. The weight of the water above a person standing at the bottom of Challenger Deep would be the same as fifty jumbo jets.[3] Yet even here, scientists have found life.[4]

Seamounts

The bottom of the Pacific Ocean is dotted with seamounts. These cone-shaped mountains are inactive volcanoes. There are more than 1,500 seamounts in the Pacific.[5] Many are found in chains. The Emperor Seamounts is the world's longest chain. It extends about 3,700 miles (5,955 kilometers) across the floor of the Pacific. This is farther than the distance across the United States.

Mountains

There are also several mountain ranges on the bottom of the Pacific. Most are in the western half of the sea. They run in a general north-to-south direction. Some of the higher peaks break through the ocean's surface. These are islands.

One Pacific mountain range is part of a longer chain that runs through many oceans. The portion in the Pacific is called the East Pacific Rise. The East Pacific Rise runs from north to south in the southeastern part of the ocean. It plays an important part in a geological theory called

Mountains Under the Sea
By Michael Tennesen
Photographs by Norbert Wu

Biologists, divers, photographers, fishermen and conservationists are all being drawn to the ocean's highest ground

LIKE THE TIPS of icebergs, the tropical Revillagigedos Islands only hint at what is lurking just beneath the sea. Tiny specks of land 360 miles south of the southern tip of Mexico's Baja California, they are the visible peaks of an underwater mountain chain known as the Eastern Pacific Rise that stretches all the way to Antarctica, hidden just below the Pacific's blue surface.

NUTRIENT-RICH WATERS and concentrations of plankton churned up by currents and upwellings support a multitude of species near undersea mountains, or seamounts. Above a manta ray with a remora attached above its eye shares an outcrop with a diver in the Revillagigedos.

These seamounts, as the underwater landmasses are known, are havens for Pacific migratory fish and mammals including whale sharks, sailfish, blue marlin, dolphins, humpback whales, tuna and hammerhead sharks. Increasingly, as with other seamounts across the world, they have also become the hangouts for marine biologists, who are only just beginning to unravel many scientific secrets hidden in an unusual dynamic of seas and currents. At the same time, seamounts have drawn the attention

🔺 *Undersea mountains support a great deal of life with nutrient-rich water and high plankton populations.*

plate tectonics. According to plate tectonics, the earth's crust sits on thirty huge pieces of rock. Each rock is called a plate.

The East Pacific Rise runs between the Pacific Plate and the Nazca Plate. Powerful forces inside the earth are pulling these two plates apart. As they spread, red-hot magma (molten rock) from deep within the earth rises and fills the gap. When the magma cools it becomes rock. This is called seafloor spreading. Scientists estimate that the East Pacific Rise spreads about six inches (fifteen centimeters) a year.[6]

However, the Pacific Ocean is not growing. It is getting smaller. As new seafloor forms, old seafloor is pushed into one of the Pacific's deep trenches. This is called subduction.

▷ Volcanoes

A volcano is an opening in the earth's surface where magma erupts. Three fourths of all the earth's volcanoes are in the Pacific Ocean.[7] Most are along the edge of the Pacific and Nazca plates. This belt of volcanic activity is known as the Ring of Fire.

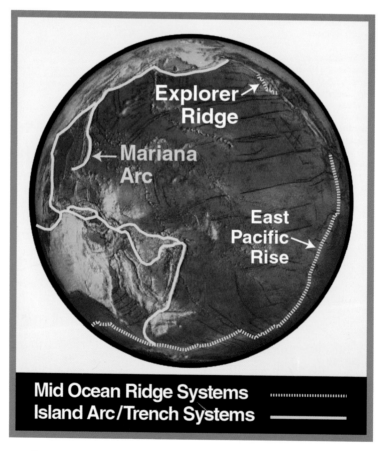

Mid Ocean Ridge Systems
Island Arc/Trench Systems

▲ The Ring of Fire circles the Pacific Ocean. The ridge and trench systems shown here complete the ring.

Each time magma erupts and cools, a volcano grows higher. Some volcanoes become so tall, they break through the ocean's surface to become a volcanic island.

All of the Hawaiian Islands are volcanic islands. Most are now inactive. Mauna Loa, though, still erupts. It is on the island of Hawaii.

In addition, a new volcanic island is being formed in the Pacific. Lo'ihi Seamount is near Hawaii. Scientists predict it will continue erupting until it has grown another 3,280 feet (1,000 meters). At this point, it will poke through the surface of the sea. Experts say this will happen in about thirty thousand years.[8]

Earthquakes

Nearly all of the earth's major earthquakes also occur along the Ring of Fire.[9] These quakes are not often felt on land, but sometimes they set off huge waves called tsunamis. Tsunamis that reach land can be deadly. Volcanoes can also cause tsunamis.

Hydrothermal Vents

In 1976, scientists discovered hydrothermal vents on the floor of the Pacific. Hydrothermal vents are places where hot water from inside the earth shoots through cracks in the ocean floor. The water, colored gray by sulfur, can be as hot as 760°F (404°C).[10] As the sulfur settles, it builds chimney-like structures from which the gray water continues to erupt. These are also called black smokers.

Hydrothermal vents, earthquakes, erupting volcanoes, subduction, and seafloor spreading are all changing the bottom of the Pacific Ocean. Yet change here is nothing new. It has been going on for millions of years. It will continue to do so for millions to come.

Chapter 4

AN OCEAN OF LIFE

One common ocean plant is seaweed. There is a wide variety of seaweed. Some are tiny, while others grow to 205 feet (62 meters) in length.[1]

The Pacific Ocean is also full of plants called phytoplankton. Phytoplankton are so tiny they can only be seen with a microscope.[2] Like plants on Earth, phytoplankton use the sun to make food. Therefore, they drift with the ocean's waves and currents in the upper waters of the ocean where sunshine can penetrate.

▲ The purple striped jellyfish is a type of zooplankton found in the Pacific Ocean.

 The pygmy goby is the smallest fish in the Pacific Ocean. They are smaller than some of the rocks on the ocean floor.

Zooplankton

There are animals that drift about with the currents, too. They are called zooplankton. Several are microscopic. The giant drifting jellyfish, however, can grow up to twenty-five feet (eight meters) long.[3] Together, the zooplankton and phytoplankton make up what is called the plankton. The plankton provide food for numerous marine animals.

Fish

Thousands of different kinds of fish live in the Pacific.[4] The smallest is the pygmy goby. It is smaller than a person's fingertip. The largest is the forty-foot-(twelve-meter) long whale shark. Pacific fish can be broad and flat like

▲ *A young white shark preys on fish, rays, and other sharks. As it gets older, the white shark feeds on larger sea mammals, such as sea lions, seals, and whales.*

the ocean sunfish, which looks like a pancake. Or they can be long and streamlined such as the barracuda.

Many fish have developed ways to outwit predators. The flying fish, for example, throws itself out of the ocean when danger approaches. It spreads its fins and sails through the air to safety.

Most Pacific fish stay close to land. The largest and fastest live in the upper 600 feet (183 meters) of water. Water up to this depth is well lit by the sun. Below this level sunlight begins to fade. This area is known as the midwater zone. It extends to 3,000 feet (914 meters). Nearly all of the fish that live here are small. The water below the midwater zone is cold and dark. Yet fish live here, too. Many deep-sea dwellers have large eyes. Some have special organs that glow like lights.

Crustaceans, Echinoderms, and Mollusks

There are other groups of animals that live in the ocean. One called crustaceans includes crabs, lobsters, and shrimp. Crustaceans have jointed legs and hard shells.

Another kind of Pacific animal is the echinoderm. Starfish, sand dollars, and sea urchins are echinoderms. Mollusks make up another group of ocean life. The most common mollusks are snails, clams, and octopus.

Mammals

Various whale species live in the Pacific. The smallest of these are the dolphins and porpoises. These animals are playful and intelligent.

▲ *The purple shoreline crab is a crustacean native to the Pacific Ocean.*

▲ *Unlike most sea mammals, the sea otter has a thick coat of fur (rather than blubber) to keep itself warm. These animals are endangered due to oil spills, and from getting caught in shell fishermen's netting.*

The largest Pacific whale species is also the largest animal on Earth. It is the blue whale. Blue whales can grow to be 100 feet (30 meters) long and weigh 200 tons (181 metric tons). This is more than the weight of thirty-two elephants. Oddly enough, these huge animals live on tiny marine animals called krill.

The Pacific is home to other whales, too. Many, such as the gray whale and the humpback whale, stay in northern waters during the summer and swim south each fall. In the spring they return north. This movement from place to place is called migration.

Not all Pacific whales migrate. Sperm whales stay in warm waters all year. Orcas, or killer whales, like cool waters.

Sea otters also like cool waters. They are unique to the northern Pacific. They can stay underwater for four minutes while looking for clams, their favorite food. Otters eat and sleep while floating on their backs.

Seals live in the Pacific, too. Northern fur seals stay in the water eight months of the year.

Birds

Several birds also spend much of their lives on the sea. They eat fish and sleep on the water. The albatross, for example, comes to land for only a few weeks each year.

Coral

The Pacific Ocean is made up of several ecosystems. An ecosystem is a group of plants and animals that live together and depend on one another to survive.

One Pacific ecosystem is based on a tiny animal called a polyp. Polyps live in warm waters. These one-inch animals attach themselves to each other, creating constantly growing communities. Each polyp takes calcium out of seawater and uses it to build a skeleton. When a polyp dies, its soft body decays, but the skeleton remains. This formation is called coral. Coral structures get bigger as polyps reproduce and die.

Coral grows in a huge variety of fantastic shapes and colors. Some look like fans, while others resemble tree branches. One kind of coral looks like mushrooms and another like deer antlers. Corals can be bright orange, yellow, purple, and green. There are about 450 different kinds of coral in the South Pacific.[5]

Coral can grow so big it creates an underwater ridge. This is called a coral reef. The Great Barrier Reef is the largest coral reef in the world. It stretches for 1,250 miles

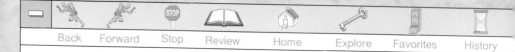

▲ Tiny organisms called polyps attach themselves together to form brightly colored mushroom coral in the Pacific Ocean.

(2,012 kilometers) along the eastern coast of Australia. It has been growing for millions of years.

Over one hundred thousand different kinds of plants and animals live around coral reefs.[6] Many fish live on the plants that grow around the coral. These fish are brightly colored and striped or spotted. Their brilliant colors and unique patterns protect them from predators. The names of these fish often describe their looks. For example, the butterfly fish has wide fins that look similar to wings. The parrotfish is bright blue. Some of the fish have unusual names. The humuhumunukunukuapuaa, for instance, is a fish common to the waters around Hawaii.

The plant-eating fish attract meat eaters. Barracudas, moray eels, and shark are often found around coral reefs.

There is even a fish that eats coral. It is called the bumphead parrotfish.

Vent Communities

Another Pacific ecosystem lives around hydrothermal vents. It is built on a unique bacteria. This bacteria uses the sulfur that comes from the vents as food. Huge clams and ten-foot- (three-meter-) long tube worms eat the bacteria. Crustaceans eat these clams and tubeworms. Fish eat the crustaceans. Hundreds of different animal species have been found around the vents. More are being discovered all of the time.[7]

Ocean Ecosystem

There are many other small ecosystems in the Pacific. Yet they all belong to one large ecosystem—that of the entire

▲ From the sky, you can see the coral reefs through the blue water of the Pacific Ocean.

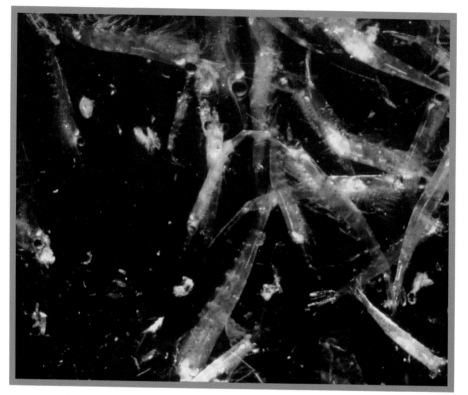

Krill play a very important role in the Pacific Ocean's ecosystem. These protein-rich, shrimplike animals are a kind of plankton that make up a large part of the diets of fish, seals, whales, and other animals.

ocean. Plankton provides food for thousands of marine species. These animals become food for others who, in turn, are eaten by larger predators. When uneaten animals die, their bodies sink and become food for the bottom dwellers. Bodies that are not eaten decay into minerals that are carried to the surface by currents. These minerals are food for the plankton.

The Pacific Ocean is huge, but it is a delicately balanced system. When one element is disturbed, all elements are affected. Each lifeform must stay healthy, therefore, if the entire ocean is to flourish.

OCEAN EXPLORATION

The people who first explored the Pacific Ocean came from Southeast Asia. These adventurers paddled out onto the sea more than two thousand years ago and discovered the islands near their homes. Then, by venturing from one island to the next, they found and settled distant islands. They may have gone as far east as Easter Island, which is about two thousand miles (3,218 km) west of Santiago, Chile.

Scientists believe that by A.D. 1000 people lived on nearly all of the major islands of the Pacific. They raised families, built towns, and developed civilizations. Their descendants still live on the islands today.

▶ European Exploration

Europeans discovered the eastern side of the Pacific in 1513. That year, Spanish explorer Vasco Núñez de Balboa sighted the ocean from a mountain in Central America.

Portuguese explorer Ferdinand Magellan led the first European expedition to sail across its waters. Magellan left Spain in 1519. His fleet traveled across the Atlantic Ocean and around the southern tip of South America. In 1520, he sailed out onto the Pacific. Its waters were so calm, Magellan called the ocean "*mare pacifico*," meaning peaceful sea. The Pacific Ocean was named.

Magellan traveled across the Pacific for ninety-eight days before finding the inhabited island of Guam. He then sailed to the Philippine Islands. There, Magellan was

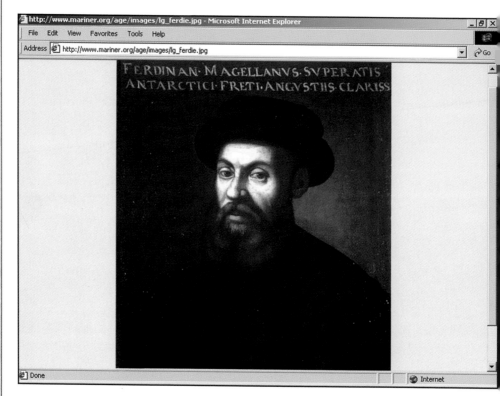

FERDINAN· MAGELLANVS· SVPERATIS
ANTARCTICI·FRETI·ANGVSTIIS·CLARISS

▲ *Ferdinand Magellan was born in 1480. In 1520, he led the first expedition across the Pacific Ocean.*

killed in a fight between native peoples. His crew returned to Spain in one of his ships in 1522.

Magellan and his crew were the first Europeans to see several of the Pacific islands. In addition, his expedition proved it was possible to sail around the earth.

Another great Pacific explorer was James Cook from England. In 1768, Cook set sail for the island of Tahiti. He was taking scientists there so they could to watch the planet Venus pass between the earth and the sun. He was also on a mission to look for what was then an unknown southern continent now known as Antarctica.[1] Cook looked for the unknown continent once more in 1772. Again, he was unable to get past the ice that covers the Southern Ocean. Cook's last voyage was in 1776. This time he searched for a northern sea route between Asia and Europe. Instead, he found the islands of Hawaii.

During his three voyages, Cook sailed farther south than any explorer before him. He was the first European to visit New Zealand and many other Pacific islands. He also mapped more of the Pacific Ocean than any explorer before him. Because of Cook's work, world maps had to be redrawn.

Exploring the Depths

By the early 1800s, most of the Pacific and its islands had been charted. Yet, ocean exploration had just begun. Now scientists wondered what was below the sea.

The bottom of the Pacific was first studied in 1874 by scientists aboard the British ship *Challenger*. They took water samples from the seafloor, and they studied deep-sea organisms.

During the 1930s, sonar helped scientists map the ocean bottom. Sound waves were shot at the seafloor. Scientists calculated ocean depth by measuring how long it took for the sound to return to the surface.

Exploring the deep ocean in person was impossible until 1930. That year, scientists invented a craft called a bathysphere. The bathysphere was a small, steel sphere designed for exploring the depths. The sphere was attached to a ship by a long, heavy cable. Two people could sit inside and look out small portholes as it was lowered into the sea.

In 1947, the bathyscaphe was invented. It was first tested the following year. The bathysphere was much like

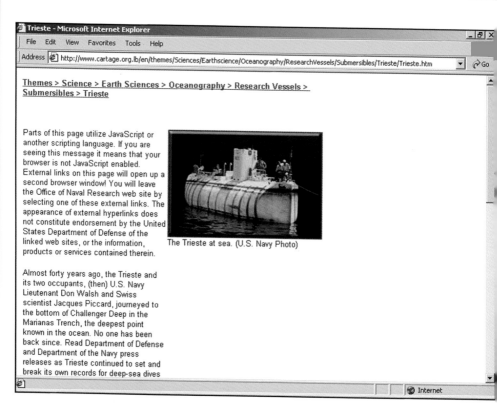

Themes > Science > Earth Sciences > Oceanography > Research Vessels > Submersibles > Trieste

Parts of this page utilize JavaScript or another scripting language. If you are seeing this message it means that your browser is not JavaScript enabled. External links on this page will open up a second browser window! You will leave the Office of Naval Research web site by selecting one of these external links. The appearance of external hyperlinks does not constitute endorsement by the United States Department of Defense of the linked web sites, or the information, products or services contained therein.

The Trieste at sea. (U.S. Navy Photo)

Almost forty years ago, the Trieste and its two occupants, (then) U.S. Navy Lieutenant Don Walsh and Swiss scientist Jacques Piccard, journeyed to the bottom of Challenger Deep in the Marianas Trench, the deepest point known in the ocean. No one has been back since. Read Department of Defense and Department of the Navy press releases as Trieste continued to set and break its own records for deep-sea dives

Don Walsh, a U.S. Navy Lieutenant, and Swiss scientist Jacques Piccard ventured to the depths of the Pacific in a mini-submarine called the Trieste. Walsh and Piccard are the only people to have reached the bottom of Challenger Deep.

the bathysphere except that it could move up and down in the water by itself.

In 1960, Jacques Piccard and United States Navy Lieutenant Don Walsh took a bathyscaphe named the *Trieste* into the Mariana Trench. They were the first people to go to the bottom of Challenger Deep.[2]

Today's underwater craft are called submersibles. Submersibles have space for a crew and sophisticated research instruments. They can be steered through the ocean at great depths while gathering all sorts of information.

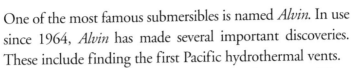

One of the most famous submersibles is named *Alvin.* In use since 1964, *Alvin* has made several important discoveries. These include finding the first Pacific hydrothermal vents.

Some submersibles move about on their own. They send information back to oceanographers working above the sea. Submersibles have helped scientists discover the immense variety of life at the bottom of the Pacific.

Satellite Technology

The latest tool to aid ocean exploration is the satellite. Satellites can measure the speed and direction of wind on the ocean. They can detect heat and chemical changes on the sea's surface. Scientists hope that one day they will be able to use this information to predict changes in the weather and climate.[3]

Oceanographers have learned a lot about the ocean over the past few centuries. Yet there is still much about the sea that is unknown. According to one marine scientist, Ellen J. Prager, "95 percent of the ocean remains to be explored."[4]

A HEALTHY SEA

A healthy ocean is important. Sea resources make our lives better. Ocean temperatures affect weather around the world. Life everywhere depends on ocean waters to keep the water cycle moving.[1] Yet in spite of our need for a healthy sea, humans are destroying parts of the Pacific.

One of the biggest threats to the Pacific is pollution. Almost half of all ocean pollution comes by way of rivers that empty into the sea.[2] Pollution is not always

▲ The Pacific Ocean provides many important resources, however, it is also good for recreational activities. With some of the biggest waves in the world, Hawaii is known as an excellent place for surfing the Pacific.

severe enough to kill large animals. However, it often kills plankton, ruining entire ecosystems.

Pollution

Sewage such as human waste is one of the most common pollutants. Even treated sewage contains material that is harmful to marine life. Chemicals are another frequent pollutant. Some come from factories. Certain chemicals reduce the amount of oxygen in ocean water. This kills the marine life that need oxygen to breathe.

Farmers use chemicals, too. Some are washed to the sea by rain. One especially dangerous chemical is DDT. Animals exposed to DDT can be killed instantly. Yet even when animals survive DDT exposure, the chemical stays in their tissues. It is passed on to any animal that eats one of them. An animal that eats several poisoned animals can receive enough small doses of DDT to cause it to die.

Lead, mercury, and copper are also finding their way into the ocean. These, too, are not always immediately dangerous. Like DDT, though, they build to lethal levels through the food chain.

Oil is another common pollutant. Most oil in the Pacific comes from spills on land. In addition, offshore wells and oil tankers sometimes leak oil into the ocean.

At times, oil tankers have large spills. One of the Pacific's worst spills happened off the coast of Alaska. In 1989, a tanker named the *Exxon Valdez* spilled nearly 11 million gallons (42 million liters) of oil.[3] This Alaskan spill killed five thousand sea otters, three hundred seals, twenty-two orcas, and thousands of other marine animals.[4] A few species have rebuilt their populations. Many have not.

Trash is also polluting the ocean. Animals get tangled and die in old fishing nets, soda cans, and plastics people

OIL SPILL FACTS >

Photos of the *Exxon Valdez* Oil Spill

Back to Spill Photos Page

Oiled loon on shore.

▲ The Exxon Valdez *oil spill was devastating to life in and around the Pacific Ocean.*

throw into the water. Much of this garbage will float around for centuries before decaying.

▶ Overfishing

Overfishing is the second serious threat to the health of the Pacific Ocean. An area is overfished when fish do not reproduce as fast as they are caught. Numerous areas of the Pacific are overfished.[5] This means that there are fewer fish in places where they once thrived.[6]

Overfishing has several causes. First, more people are fishing Pacific waters than ever before. In addition, many

fishermen and women use huge nets, some nearly thirty miles (forty-eight kilometers) long.[7] These nets kill all of the animals that wander into them. Many are not even wanted by the fishermen and are thrown back into the sea. Each year twenty thousand dolphins are accidentally killed by the nets of United States tuna fishermen.[8]

One partial solution to overfishing could be aquaculture. This is a method of raising fish, much like farmers raise crops and livestock. Many Asian countries have large aquaculture farms.[9]

Depletion

Overfishing and pollution have led to the depletion of numerous marine animals. A species is depleted when its population becomes very low. Some Pacific fish listed as depleted are the ocean perch, king crab, shrimp, and cod.[10]

Depletion of a species can upset the balance of an entire ecosystem. Furthermore, depletion can lead to a species' extinction.

Endangered Species

Some Pacific species are already endangered. This means there are so few of the animal alive they may become extinct. Pacific animals listed as endangered include sea lions, sea otters, seals, turtles, and whales.[11]

In an effort to help these animals build back their populations, laws have been made to protect them. It is illegal to disturb or harm any animal on the endangered list. This has helped rebuild some species. For example, the gray whale was close to extinction just fifty years ago. Then laws were made to keep it from being hunted. Now there are more than twenty thousand gray whales around the globe.[12]

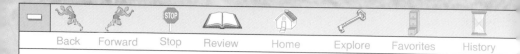

▲ The health of the ocean affects everyone and everything. That is why it is so important for nations to abide by the International Law of the Sea Treaty.

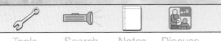

Marine sanctuaries are protecting all ocean life. A marine sanctuary is an area of the ocean where animals cannot be disturbed. Several Pacific countries, including the United States, have created these ocean parks. In fact, the second largest sanctuary in the world is off the coast of California. It is called the Monterey Bay National Marine Sanctuary.

Laws

Keeping the ocean healthy has been hard since it does not belong to any one country. For this reason, people began working through the United Nations (UN) to help the seas. The UN is an organization of people from several different countries.

The UN has worked for many years writing laws to help all of the oceans on the earth. Many of the regulations are about ocean fishing and pollution. The laws were put together in a document called the International Law of the Sea Treaty. More than 140 nations have agreed to follow the treaty.

This is a good start. If everyone obeys the Law of the Sea, the health of the Pacific Ocean will begin to improve. This is vital to us all, because a healthy earth depends on a healthy ocean.

Chapter 1. The Earth's Largest Ocean

1. Trevor Day, *Oceans* (New York: Facts On File, 1999), p. 6.

2. Natalie Goldstein, *Earth Almanac: An Annual Geophysical Review of the State of the Planet* (Phoenix: The Oryx Press, 2000), p. 188.

3. "Pacific Ocean," *The World Factbook 2002*, March 19, 2003, <http://www.cia.gov/cia/publications/factbook> (July 10, 2003).

4. Richard Ellis, *Encyclopedia of the Sea* (New York: Alfred A. Knopf, 2000), p. 245.

5. Ray Sumner, ed., *World Geography* (Pasadena, Calif.: Salem Press, Inc., 2001), p. 1,809.

6. Jeffrey S. Levinton, *Marine Biology: Function, Biodiversity, Ecology* (New York: Oxford University Press, 2001), p. 22.

7. Goldstein, p. 115.

8. Jennifer Ackerman, "New Eyes on the Oceans," *National Geographic*, October 2000, p. 95.

9. Ibid.

Chapter 2. Ocean Resources

1. Trevor Day, *Oceans* (New York: Facts On File, 1999), p. 6.

2. Ibid., p. 172.

3. Peter Ullman, Chairman, Tidal Electric, Inc., 2002, <http://www.tidalelectric.com> p. 5.

4. Richard Ellis, *Encyclopedia of the Sea* (New York: Alfred A. Knopf, 2000), p. 205.

5. Tom Garrison, *Essentials of Oceanography* (Pacific Grove, Calif.: Brooks Cole Publishing Company, 2001), p. 306.

Chapter 3. The Ocean Floor

1. Ray Sumner, ed., *World Geography* (Pasadena, Calif.: Salem Press, Inc., 2001), p. 2,085.

2. Barbara Charton, *The Facts On File Dictionary of Marine Science* (New York: Facts on File, 2001), p. 188.

3. Peter Benchley, *Ocean Planet* (New York: Harry N. Abrams, 1995), p. 102.

4. Sylvia A. Earle, *Sea Change* (New York: B. P. Putnam's Sons, 1995), p. 50.

5. Richard Ellis, *Encyclopedia of the Sea* (New York: Alfred A. Knopf, 2000), p. 303.

6. Trevor Day, *Oceans* (New York: Facts On File, 1999), p. 6.

7. Ellen J. Prager with Sylvia Earle, *The Oceans* (New York: McGraw Hill, 2000), p. 156.

8. Tom Garrison, *Essentials of Oceanography* (Pacific Grove, Calif.: Brooks Cole Publishing Company, 2001), p. 53.

9. Prager with Earle, p. 156.

10. Richard A. Lutz, "Deep Sea Vents: Science at the Extremes," *National Geographic*, October 2000, p. 118.

Chapter 4. An Ocean of Life

1. Tom Garrison, *Essentials of Oceanography* (Pacific Grove, Calif.: Brooks Cole Publishing Company, 2001), p. 274.

2. Natalie Goldstein, *Earth Almanac: An Annual Geophysical Review of the State of the Planet* (Phoenix: The Oryx Press, 2000), p. 147.

3. Ibid., p. 247.

4. Jeffrey S. Levinton, *Marine Biology: Function, Biodiversity, Ecology* (New York: Oxford University Press, 2001), p. 170.

5. David Doubilet, "Coral Eden," *National Geographic*, January 1999, p. 7.

6. Goldstein, p. 153.

7. Richard A. Lutz, "Deep Sea Vents: Science at the Extremes," *National Geographic*, October 2000, p. 119.

Chapter 5. Ocean Exploration

1. Richard Ellis, *Encyclopedia of the Sea* (New York: Alfred A. Knopf, 2000), p. 79.

2. Ibid., p. 348.

3. Jennifer Ackerman, "New Eyes on the Oceans," *National Geographic*, October 2000, p. 114.

4. Ellen J. Prager with Sylvia Earle, *The Oceans* (New York: McGraw Hill, 2000), p. 295.

Chapter 6. A Healthy Sea

1. Sylvia A. Earle, *Sea Change: A Message of the Oceans* (New York: G.P. Putnam's Sons, 1995), p. xii.

2. Tom Garrison, *Essentials of Oceanography* (Pacific Grove, Calif.: Brooks Cole Publishing Company, 2001), p. 309.

3. Earle, p. 279.

4. John G. Mitchell, "In the Wake of the Spill," *National Geographic,* March 1999, p. 106.

5. David Helvarg, *Blue Frontier: Saving America's Living Seas* (New York: W. H. Freeman and Company, 2001), p. 4.

6. Earle, pp. 186–187.

7. Jeffrey S. Levinton, *Marine Biology: Function, Biodiversity, Ecology* (New York: Oxford University Press, 2001), pp. 448–449.

8. Earle, p. 172.

9. Helvarg, pp. 173–174.

10. Natalie Goldstein, *Earth Almanac: An Annual Geophysical Review of the State of the Planet* (Phoenix: The Oryx Press, 2000), p. 120.

11. "The Pacific Ocean," *The World Factbook 2002*, March 19, 2003, <http://www.cia.gov/cia/publications/factbook> (July 10, 2003).

12. Sylvia A. Earle and Wolcott Henry, *Wild Ocean: America's Parks Under the Sea* (Washington, D.C.: National Geographic Society, 1999), p. 41.

Further Reading

Blaxland, Beth. *Mollusks: Snails, Clams, and Their Relatives.* Broomall, Penn.: Chelsea House Publishers, 2003.

Gaines, Ann Graham. *Captain Cook Explores the Pacific in World History.* Berkeley Heights, N.J.: Enslow Publishers, Inc., 2002.

Lambert, David. *The Pacific Ocean.* Austin, Tex.: Raintree Steck-Vaughn Publishers, 1997.

Meltzer, Milton. *Ferdinand Magellan: First to Sail Around the World.* Tarrytown, N.Y.: Marshall Cavendish Corporation, 2001.

Morgan, Sally. *Crabs and Crustaceans.* North Mankato, Minn.: Thameside Press, 2001.

Patent, Dorothy Hinshaw. *Shaping the Earth.* New York: Clarion Books, 2000.

Petersen, David, and Christine. *The Pacific Ocean.* New York: Children's Press, 2001.

Prevost, John F. *Pacific Ocean.* Edina, Minn.: ABDO Publishing Company, 2003.

Sayre, April Pulley. *El Niño and La Niña: Weather in the Headlines.* Brookfield, Conn.: Twenty-First Century Books, 2000.

Taylor, Leighton. *The Pacific Ocean.* Farmington Hills, Mich.: Gale Group, 1998.

Wells, Marguerite. *Coastal Zones of the Pacific: A Descriptive Atlas.* Corvallis, Ore.: Oregon Sea Grant, 1996.

Williams, Jean Kinney. *Cook: James Cook Charts the Pacific Ocean.* Minneapolis, Minn.: Compass Point Books, 2003.